The Hollywood Model

A Step-by-Step Guide to Writing Compelling Screenplays, Dramas & Stories With AI & Prompt Engineering

Phill Akinwale, M.Sc., PMP

PUBLISHER

Praizion Media

The Hollywood Model
Published by Praizion Media
P.O Box 22241, Mesa, AZ 85277
E-mail: info@praizion.com
www.praizion.com

Author
Phillip Akinwale, M.Sc., OPM3, PMP, PMI -RMP, PMI-SP, PMI-ACP, PSM, CSM

Copyright © 2023 Praizion Media

All rights reserved. No part of this publication may be reproduced, transmitted in any form or by any means including but not limited to electronic, recording, manual, mechanical, recording, photograph, photocopy, or stored in any retrieval system, without the prior written permission of the publisher.

ISBN 978-1-934579-81-7

The author and publisher make no warranties or representation that use of this publication will result in passing the PMP® exam or about the completeness and accuracy of the contents. The author and publisher accept no liability, losses or damages of any kind caused or alleged to be caused directly or indirectly by this publication.

PMI®, the PMI® logo, PMBOK® and PMP® are registered marks of the Project Management Institute, Inc. Project Management Institute, *A Guide to the Project Management Body of Knowledge (PMBOK® Guide)* Seventh Edition, Project Management Institute, Inc., 2021. Copyright and all rights reserved.

Printed in the United States of America

Dedication

I dedicate this book to all writers, filmmakers, directors producers and creatives of all genres.

Have a FUN time creating with AI!

.

Table of Contents

Chapter 1: Introduction _____ 5

Chapter 2: Prompt Engineering Models _____ 9

Chapter 3: The Hollywood Model _____ 17

Chapter 4: The BRAINS Framework _____ 26

Chapter 5: The PLOTDRAMA Model _____ 33

Chapter 6: The Power of Detailed Prompts _____ 43

Chapter 7: Exploring Boundless AI Creativity _____ 50

Chapter 9: Hands-On Workshop With Phill _____ 55

Chapter 10: Conclusion _____ 70

Appendix 1: 50 Fictional Ideas to Generate Screenplays, Books and Stories _____ 72

Appendix B: 10 Screenplay Prompts _____ 76

Appendix C: 10 Screenplay Prompts _____ 77

Appendix D: 25 Editing Prompts _____ 78

Appendix E: 10 Sizing Prompts _____ 80

About the Author _____ 81

Chapter 1: Introduction

Welcome to this book. You could title it "A Writer's Guide to Using AI for Story Writing". In this guide, we will explore the exciting intersection of creativity and technology, where artificial intelligence (AI) can be harnessed as a powerful tool to enhance your storytelling process. Whether you are a seasoned writer or just starting your journey, integrating AI into your storytelling toolkit can unlock new realms of imagination and efficiency.

The field of AI has made tremendous strides in recent years, offering innovative solutions that can assist writers in generating ideas, developing characters, refining plots, and even providing writing suggestions. By leveraging the capabilities of AI, you can unleash your creativity and take your storytelling to new heights.

This guide is designed to help you navigate the world of AI for story writing, providing valuable insights and practical tips on how to effectively incorporate AI tools into your creative process. From understanding the different AI models and techniques available to exploring the best practices for collaboration between human writers and AI algorithms, this guide aims to empower you to make the most of this cutting-edge technology.

We will journey into the benefits and considerations of using AI, including the potential to generate vast amounts of content, overcome writer's block, and explore alternative perspectives. We will also address the ethical implications and limitations of AI in storytelling, emphasizing the importance of maintaining your unique voice and creative vision while leveraging the capabilities of AI as a supportive tool.

Throughout this guide, we will provide step-by-step instructions, real-world examples, and practical exercises to help you integrate AI seamlessly into your writing process. By embracing the power of AI, you can enhance your productivity, unlock new creative possibilities, and refine your storytelling craft.

So, let's embark on this exciting journey together and discover how AI can become your trusted ally in the realm of storytelling. Get ready to unlock new dimensions of creativity and transform the way you approach writing with the Writer's Guide to Using AI for Story Writing!

1.1: Importance of Artificial Intelligence in Creative Writing

In recent years, the capabilities of Artificial Intelligence (AI) have dramatically expanded. No longer confined to the realms of data analysis and repetitive tasks, AI has started to venture into the sphere of creative writing, aiding authors in crafting narratives for fiction, drama, and movie scripts. The use of AI in writing goes beyond simple grammar corrections; it extends to concept development, plot structuring, character creation, and even crafting dialogues. By leveraging the power of AI, writers can break through creative blocks, streamline their writing processes, and produce rich and diverse narratives.

1.2: The Role of Detailed Prompts in High-Quality Content Generation

Detailed prompts are crucial tools in the creative process. They act as springboards for ideas, providing a starting point from which writers can weave intricate narratives. These prompts play a significant role when working with AI for content generation. A well-crafted prompt can guide the AI, enabling it to generate content that aligns closely with the writer's intentions. By understanding and mastering the art of creating detailed prompts, writers can harness the potential of AI to produce high-quality content effectively and efficiently.

1.3: The Potential of AI to Enhance the Writing Process

AI has the potential to revolutionize the writing process. With AI's advanced algorithms and pattern recognition capabilities, it can offer fresh perspectives and unexpected plot twists, helping writers to push boundaries and step outside their creative comfort zones. Furthermore, AI can mimic various writing styles, providing writers with a diverse range of narrative voices to explore and learn from.

1.4: AI and Human-like Narratives

One of the most exciting aspects of AI in writing is its ability to create human-like narratives. The latest AI models, trained on vast amounts of data, can generate content that mirrors human thought processes, emotions, and expression. This opens up new possibilities for writers, allowing them to explore diverse narrative styles and techniques, and create compelling, human-centric stories.

1.5: The Journey Ahead

In the chapters that follow, we will journey deeper into the world of AI and writing. We'll explore how to use prompts effectively, how to harness the potential of AI to enhance your writing process, and how to create more human-like narratives. From understanding the mechanics of AI to crafting detailed prompts, this book aims to equip writers with the knowledge and tools they need to navigate the rapidly evolving landscape of AI and creative writing. Get ready to embark on a journey of exploration and discovery, where creativity and technology intertwine to create narratives that resonate with readers.

This journey of harnessing the power of AI for writing is not just about technology; it's about enhancing our creative potential and bringing our stories to life in ways we never thought possible.

Chapter 2: Prompt Engineering Models

Prompt engineering models are systematic approaches used to guide story creation. The ABCD Prompt Model is a simple and effective method for writing short stories. It stands for Action, Background, Character, and Drama.

The ABCs of Writing AI Stories

When writing a simple story, you can feed your AI tool with these basics:
- Action is the driving force of the story. It is what keeps the reader engaged and wanting to know what happens next. The action should be exciting and suspenseful, and it should move the story forward.

- Background provides context for the story. It tells the reader where and when the story takes place, and it introduces the characters and their relationships to each other. The background should be rich and detailed, but it should not slow down the action.

- Character is the heart of the story. The reader should care about the characters and want to see them succeed. The characters should be believable and relatable, and they should have clear motivations.

- Drama is what makes the story interesting. It is the conflict that the characters face, and it is what drives the story forward. The drama should be believable and relatable, and it should keep the reader engaged.

The ABCD prompt for AI writing is a simple and effective method for writing short stories. It can be used to write a wide variety of stories, from thrillers to comedies to romances. If you are looking to write a short story, the ABCD of Writing is a great place to start. Just fill it in like a form and paste it into your AI tool of choice and see it do the magic!

2.1: Understanding Prompt Engineering Models for Story Writing

Whether you're crafting a short story, penning a novel, or scripting a play or movie, these next three models provide a structured pathway to bring your ideas to life.

This chapter introduces three prompt engineering models: the HOLLYWOOD model, the BRAINS model, and the PLOTDRAMA model. Each offers a unique perspective on story crafting.

2.2: The HOLLYWOOD Model

Named after the home of storytelling magic, the HOLLYWOOD model lays out a comprehensive process for crafting compelling narratives. Each letter of the mnemonic corresponds to a crucial phase of story development:

- **H**: Hook (Intro): Your story should start with an event, a dialogue, or a scenario that piques the reader's interest and immediately draws them into your world.
- **O**: Origin (Background): Here, you create the world in which your story unfolds. It's the backstory, setting, and context for your narrative.
- **L**: Lead (Characters): The protagonists, antagonists, and supporting characters come alive at this stage. Develop their traits, desires, fears, and motivations.
- **L**: Layout (Plot): It's where you map out your story's main events. Each event should logically flow from the previous one, forming an interconnected chain that moves the plot forward.
- **Y**: Yield (The Punch): This is the turning point. The moment that changes everything, propelling your story towards its climax.
- **W**: Wave (The Drama): Now you add the emotional meat of your story. Here, the conflict escalates, creating suspense and tension that keeps your readers engaged.
- **O**: Ovation (High Points): This is the climax. The point of highest emotional intensity. It's where the story's main conflict reaches its peak.
- **O**: Outcome (Closing): After the climax, you resolve the conflict and start tying up loose ends, leading your narrative towards a satisfying conclusion.
- **D**: Detail Review: Finally, review each element of your story for consistency, pacing, character development, and overall narrative arc.

2.3: The BRAINS Model

While HOLLYWOOD provides a comprehensive structure, the BRAINS model focuses more on the essential elements of storytelling:

- **B**: Background: The setting, time, and context for your story.
- **R**: Roles: Your characters and their motivations.
- **A**: Action: The events that form the plot and engage your reader.
- **I**: Introspection: Insights into your characters' thoughts and feelings.
- **N**: Next steps: The build-up of suspense and anticipation for what's to come.
- **S**: Solution: The resolution of the conflict and the story's conclusion.

2.4: The PLOTDRAMA Model

Our third model, PLOTDRAMA, focuses on the narrative's dramatic and plot-driven elements:

- **P**: Premise: The core concept that drives your story.
- **L**: Lore: The world-building and background details.
- **O**: Outline: The key plot points in your narrative.
- **T**: Twists: Unexpected turns that keep readers engaged.
- **D**: Drama: Emotional conflict and tension.
- **R**: Resolution: The climax and conflict resolution.
- **A**: Action: Significant character-driven events that advance the story.
- **M**: Moment of Triumph: The climactic triumph of the protagonist.
- **A**: Aftermath: Wrapping up loose ends and resolving plot twists.

Each of these models provides a roadmap for writers to explore, experiment with, and eventually master the art of crafting engaging narratives. The choice of model depends on your unique writing style and the nature of the story you wish to tell.

COMPARING THE MODELS

Here's an expanded matrix with more detailed pros and cons for each model:

BRAINS Model

Pros:

- **Brevity:** The BRAINS model is simple and to-the-point, making it a great choice for beginners or writers who prefer a less complicated approach to storytelling.
- **Well-rounded:** It covers all key elements of storytelling, ensuring a balanced narrative that doesn't neglect character development, plot progression, or background.
- **Versatility:** This model can be used for any kind of fiction writing, from short stories to novels, allowing for creative freedom.

Cons:

- **Lacks Specificity:** While the BRAINS model covers the general aspects of storytelling, it might not provide a detailed guide for structuring the sequence of events or the development of tension and climaxes.
- **Limited Guidance:** Its simplicity, while a strength in some regards, may lack the guidance required for more intricate narratives.

PLOTDRAMA Model

Pros:

- **Emphasizes Drama:** As the name suggests, this model ensures that your story has a compelling narrative arc, complete with high points, major turning points, and a satisfying resolution.
- **Structured:** Provides a clear structure to follow, ensuring a well-organized plot and making it suitable for complex narratives.

- **Intrigue and Depth:** This model encourages writers to include significant moments that add depth and intrigue to the story, enriching the reader's experience.

Cons:

- **Complexity:** The DRAMATIC PLOT model, while comprehensive, might be overwhelming for beginner writers or for those who prefer a simpler narrative structure.
- **Less Flexibility:** Might not be as suitable for stories with a non-linear plot or unconventional narrative structure, as it strongly emphasizes a traditional narrative arc.

HOLLYWOOD Model

Pros:

- **Complete Storytelling Model:** The HOLLYWOOD model ensures that every aspect of storytelling is covered, from the introduction to a detailed review of all elements.
- **Engaging Narrative:** It emphasizes an engaging narrative throughout, ensuring that the story is captivating from start to finish.
- **Builds Tension:** This model guides the writer through building suspense and tension effectively, enhancing the story's emotional impact.

Cons:

- **Overly Structured:** Some writers may find the HOLLYWOOD model too rigid for their storytelling style. It's especially suited for traditional narratives and may not cater to more experimental forms of storytelling.
- **Detailed:** While its comprehensive nature can be a boon for some, beginner writers or those who prefer a more flexible framework may find it overwhelming.

All these models have their unique strengths and weaknesses. The choice depends on the nature of the story, the style of the writer, and the intended impact on the audience.

Model	Pros	Cons
BRAINS	Brevity, Well-rounded, Versatility	Lacks Specificity, Limited Guidance
PLOTDRAMA	Emphasizes Drama, Structured, Intrigue	Complexity, Less Flexibility
HOLLYWOOD	Complete Storytelling Model, Engaging Narrative, Builds Tension	Overly Structured, Detailed

Chapter 3: The Hollywood Model

The Hollywood Model is a writing framework that was developed in his book The Hollywood Model: A Step-by-Step Guide to Writing a Compelling Story With AI. The model is based on the idea that all successful stories follow a similar structure, which I call the "Hollywood Formula."

The Human Element

As a writer of over 2 dozen books, comics, film-shorts, and dramas, I know that the key to a great story is the human element. The audience needs to connect with the characters and feel their emotions. AI can be a great tool for generating ideas and structuring stories, screen-plays and dramas, but it can't replace the human touch!

That's why I'm excited about the Hollywood Model. This model takes real facts and situations that you have organically come up with and puts them into a structured story. This allows you to get the best of both worlds: the creativity and insights of AI, combined with the human touch that makes stories resonate with audiences.

Here's how it works:

1. Start with a real-world situation. This could be anything from a news story to a personal experience.
2. Break down the situation into its component parts. Who are the characters? What are their goals? What are the obstacles they face?
3. Use the Hollywood Model to structure your story. This will help you create a compelling narrative with the right amount of tension and release.
4. Add your own unique voice. This is where the human element comes in. What do you want to say with your story? What insights do you have to share?

The Hollywood Model is a powerful tool that can help you write better stories. If you're just starting out as a writer, or a seasoned Hollywood pro, I encourage you to give it a try!

Here are some additional insights about how to use AI to create more human stories:

- Don't be afraid to experiment. AI is a new tool, and there's no one right way to use it. Experiment with different techniques and see what works best for you.
- Be mindful of the limitations of AI. AI can't replace the human touch. It can generate ideas and help you structure your story, but it can't create characters that feel real or emotions that resonate with audiences.

- Use AI as a collaborator, not a replacement. AI can be a great partner in the writing process. It can help you generate ideas, brainstorm solutions, and improve your work. But it's important to remember that AI is just a tool. It's up to you to use it to create stories that are both human and engaging.

3.1: The Breakdown of the Hollywood Model

The Hollywood Model is an effective framework for constructing a captivating narrative, favored by filmmakers and writers alike for its comprehensive approach. Let's examine the HOLLYWOOD mnemonic using our character, Phill, and his thrilling escape story.

3.2: Hook: Captivating the Audience

The initial 'H' stands for Hook, an immediate incident or situation that serves to grab the audience's attention. For our story, Phill finds himself in the midst of a robbery scene that he narrowly escapes. This sudden action establishes the tone of the story and instantly pulls the audience into Phill's high-stakes world.

3.3: Origin: Setting the Stage

Origin, the 'O,' refers to the backstory and setting. Here we detail the environment Phill operates in. Perhaps Phill is a reformed criminal trying to lead an honest life, or maybe he's an innocent man in the wrong place at the wrong time. Providing such context offers a deeper understanding of the character and the nature of his world.

3.4: Lead: Defining Characters

The first 'L' signifies Lead, where we get into the characterization of Phill. We define his traits, his motivations, and his fears. If Phill is an ex-convict, we need to know what led him to crime in the first place and what is driving his pursuit for change. By developing a well-rounded character, we encourage audience empathy and engagement.

3.5: Layout: Plotting the Course

Layout, the second 'L,' pertains to the plot of the story. It involves charting the course Phill will follow from the robbery scene through the alley and beyond. Each event should be connected logically, forming a coherent progression that the audience can follow.

3.6: Yield: The Turning Point

'Yield,' denoted by 'Y,' signifies the turning point of the story. In Phill's case, it might be an encounter in the alley - perhaps with a former criminal acquaintance or a potential ally. This confrontation becomes a pivot that changes the course of Phill's escape and propels the story towards its climax.

3.7: Wave: Building the Drama

The first 'O' stands for 'Wave,' representing the buildup of drama and tension. As Phill navigates the complex scenario, we weave in various challenges and conflicts. His decisions and their consequences keep the audience on the edge of their seats.

3.8: Ovation: The Climax

'Ovation,' the second 'O,' signifies the climax. This is the peak moment where Phill must confront the most significant conflict of the story. Maybe Phill is cornered and must face a difficult choice between reverting to his old criminal habits or risk getting caught while retaining his newly-found morality.

3.9: Outcome: The Resolution

The 'D' stands for 'Outcome,' indicating the resolution of the story. This is where we conclude Phill's escape journey. Whether he escapes successfully or gets caught, the outcome must feel satisfying to the audience, resolving the tension and conflict that's been built up.

3.10: Detail Review: The Final Touch

Finally, the second 'D' represents the 'Detail Review.' At this stage, we scrutinize the narrative for coherence, pacing, and character development. We ensure that every detail is in place, from the consistency of Phill's actions with his character traits to the natural progression of the plot. In essence, the Hollywood model provides a structured, comprehensive approach to crafting compelling narratives. With its help, Phill's escape turns from a simple sequence of events into a suspenseful, character-driven narrative, full of dramatic tension and engaging story beats.

Chapter 3.11: Crafting the Story: A Scaled Version

Let's explore the Hollywood model in action with a more fleshed-out narrative.

Hook: Our story begins with a bang. Phill, an innocent bystander, finds himself entangled in a dangerous situation. A group of heavily armed men have launched an assault in Trewaba, a bustling city in West Africa. Phill, who is merely 10 feet away from the chaos, watches in horror as the armed men target a frantic driver in a Mercedes Benz.

Origin: Prior to this day, Phill lived an unassuming life in Trewaba. He is a kind man, well-loved by his community, a person who had never expected to find himself in such a deadly situation.

Lead: Phill is a man of determination and courage. While others may cower in fear, Phill finds himself propelled by a need to survive and help those in danger, including the Mercedes driver.

Layout: As the story unfolds, Phill takes strategic steps to evade the armed men and help the besieged driver. He ducks behind a series of crates, intending to draw some attention away from the Mercedes.

Yield: The turning point occurs when Phill finds an old, rusted pipe. He takes a calculated risk, using it to create a diversion. He throws the pipe across the alley, drawing the attention of one of the armed men.

Wave: As Phill dashes through the maze-like alleyways of Trewaba, the tension escalates. The armed men, now aware of Phill's presence, are hot on his trail. Phill's heart races, mirroring the pace of the story.

Ovation: The climax hits when Phill, exhausted and cornered, finds unexpected aid. A group of Trewaba locals, having noticed the chase, intervene. Using a series of homemade distractions, they provide Phill with an escape route.

Outcome: As the locals distract the gunmen, Phill makes his escape, disappearing into Trewaba's twisting, narrow streets. He finds refuge in a hidden corner of the city, heart pounding, safe at last.

Detail Review: Looking back, we ensure the story's coherence. Phill's actions align with his character, demonstrating bravery and quick thinking. The progression of events is logical and the narrative tension palpable, leading to a satisfying resolution.

By incorporating the Hollywood model into our narrative, we're able to craft a rich, engaging story. Phill's harrowing escape from danger is more than just a sequence of events—it's a gripping narrative filled with tension, character development, and dramatic climaxes. This framework allows us to transform a simple story into a compelling cinematic experience.

The Story

Here is a scaled-down version of the story (which if I might add, is based on a real-life event!) Phill, an unassuming man living in the bustling city of Trewaba, West Africa, was caught in the crossfire of a gang of armed men attacking a driver in a Mercedes Benz. Phill knew he had to do something, so he pushed past his fear and ran towards the car. He ducked behind a series of crates, intending to draw some attention away from the driver. As he hid, he took a deep breath and tried to calm his racing heart.

Phill knew he couldn't stay hidden for long. He had to do something to help the driver. He scanned the alleyway for something he could use as a weapon. He spotted an old, rusted pipe and picked it up. Phill took a deep breath and stepped out from behind the crates. He threw the pipe across the alleyway, hoping to create a diversion. As the pipe clattered to the ground, the men turned their attention to Phill.

Phill took off running. He darted through the maze-like alleyways of Trewaba, the men hot on his heels. His heart pounded in his chest as he ran for his life. Phill was exhausted and cornered. He knew he couldn't outrun the men. He turned to face them, raising the pipe as a weapon. Suddenly, a group of Trewaba locals appeared. They had seen the chase and had come to Phill's aid. The locals began to shout and throw objects at the men, distracting them. Phill took the opportunity to escape. He ran as fast as he could, disappearing into the twisting, narrow streets of Trewaba. He found refuge in a hidden corner of the city, heart pounding, safe at last.

Phill looked back on the events of the day. He had been lucky to escape with his life. But he knew he would never forget the courage of the Trewaba locals who had come to his aid.

Chapter 3: HOLLYWOOD Model Assignment:

1. Develop a comprehensive screenplay using the HOLLYWOOD model as your guide.
2. Utilize the HOLLYWOOD worksheet to meticulously flesh out the Hook, Origin, Lead, Layout, Yield, Wave, Ovation, Outcome, and Detail Review aspects of your narrative.
3. Upon completion of your detailed outline, proceed to transform it into the first draft of your enthralling screenplay.
4. Remember, your worksheet will serve as your roadmap to navigate the complex and fascinating world you are about to create.
5. When you have filled out the entire worksheet, proceed to write a detailed screenplay of your novel based on these elements.
6. Now feed in the contents of the sheet by copying and pasting the table (from Excel), Word or other tool directly into ChatGPT or Google Bard, before pressing "ENTER" include the prompt: "WRITE A DETAILED SCREENPLAY BASED ON THESE PARAMETERS".
7. Try this with the latest version of ChatGPT and Google Bard. Compare results.
8. Which result is better? Yours, ChatGPT or Google Bard?

How Long Should The Story Be?

Always include sizing information eventually as you write your final prompts. Number of words and or chapters! The more chapters, the more iterations advised and the more you should decompose, writing piecemeal, chapter by chapter. This gets the AI tools super-focused on just one quality-written chapter at a time. It is a great way of writing large stories while upholding quality levels.

THE HOLLYWOOD MODEL

Element	Description
Hook (Intro)	
Origin (Background)	
Lead (Characters)	
Layout (Plot)	
Yield (The Punch)	
Wave (The Drama)	
Ovation (High Points)	
Outcome (Closing)	
Detail Review	

Chapter 4: The BRAINS Framework

The BRAINS framework, an acronym representing Background, Roles, Action, Introspection, Next Steps, and Solution, is a potent storytelling model that writers across genres can employ to craft engaging narratives. Be it a character-driven drama, an action-packed thriller, or a high-stakes heist, BRAINS provides a well-rounded structure for your tale, ensuring that each essential aspect of storytelling is addressed.

Let's examine each component of the BRAINS framework and see how we can use it to shape the second part of Phill's story.

4.1 Background

This is where we build the world and the context of our narrative. In Phill's case, our background takes us to the serene but challenging landscapes of Tibet. As Phill, still recovering from the traumatic attack, travels to this mystical land, the reader is introduced to the world of Tibetan martial arts, traditions, and the stark contrast to Phill's usual urban environment.

4.2 Roles

Here, we focus on developing characters and their motivations. Phill, our protagonist, is trying to heal and prepare for any future threat. We also introduce his Tibetan mentors, their philosophies, wisdom, and their role in Phill's transformation. The relationships he forms, the challenges he faces, all contribute to his evolution.

4.3 Action

This is the heart of the plot, where our character's decisions drive the story forward. Phill's rigorous training in martial arts and weaponry, his battles with his inner demons, his struggles and triumphs, all form the action part of our narrative. This section should be vivid, engaging, and reflective of Phill's determination and resilience.

4.4 Introspection

Here, we dive into Phill's psyche, delving into his thoughts and feelings. As he pushes his physical boundaries, Phill also grapples with his fears and the traumatic memories of the attack. This introspective journey allows readers to empathize with Phill, strengthening their emotional investment in his journey.

THE HOLLYWOOD MODEL

4.5 Next Steps

This section is all about anticipation, setting up the pieces for what's to come. As Phill completes his training, an ominous message from the past arrives, hinting at a possible resurgence of the threat he faced. This revelation leaves Phill and the readers on the edge, pondering over the next course of action.

4.6 Solution

Lastly, we conclude our story. However, given that this is the second part of a trilogy, our 'solution' might not resolve everything. Instead, it could be a 'gateway' solution leading to the final part of the trilogy. Phill, now a skilled fighter, stands at a crossroads, contemplating his next move. The story ends with a cliffhanger, leaving readers eagerly anticipating the final part of the trilogy.

Using the BRAINS model in this way provides a structured, engaging narrative, without compromising on character development or emotional depth. This approach is what gives the BRAINS framework its power - its ability to balance all the crucial components of storytelling effectively. Whether you're penning a novel or drafting a screenplay, the BRAINS framework is a reliable guide to compelling storytelling.

Now, let's create a short story that showcases scalability and creativity by putting these pieces together in a concise way. Here's a scaled-down version of Phill's story using the BRAINS model:

The Aftermath

Phill, his body aching from the wounds of a past attack, journeyed to the serene landscapes of Tibet, a stark contrast to his familiar urban life. His goal was simple yet daunting - to master martial arts and weaponry, to become strong enough to face any future threats.

Phill found himself under the tutelage of Tenzin, an aged monk with eyes gleaming with wisdom. Tenzin, along with the other monks, began molding Phill, not just in combat but also in thought.

Days melted into nights as Phill trained, his body dancing to the rhythm of the ancient martial art forms. He battled the chill of the Tibetan winters and the ghosts of his past that haunted his mind. His victories, however small, were his alone, and they cemented his resolve to fight.

During the stillness of the Tibetan nights, Phill introspected, his mind grappling with a whirlpool of thoughts. The pain of the past attack, his drive to prepare for any future threat, and the tranquility of his new life battled within him. His emotional journey deepened his bond with Tenzin and the others, allowing him to understand their teachings on a profound level.

Just as Phill started finding peace within this routine, a raven arrived carrying an ominous message. It hinted at the resurrection of the past danger that Phill had narrowly escaped. His heart pounded in his chest as he held the feathered messenger, the chill of the impending threat seeping into him.

Phill, now more prepared and determined than ever, found himself standing at the edge of the future. The serene landscapes of Tibet had forged a new version of him, a warrior ready to face any storm. The story ended with Phill, his gaze fixed on the horizon, contemplating his next move, leaving readers waiting with bated breath for the final part of this trilogy.

Chapter 4 Conclusion: Implementing the BRAINS Framework

Through our exploration of Phill's journey, we've seen how the BRAINS framework can transform a story. From setting the backdrop in the tranquil landscapes of Tibet to introducing characters such as the wise Tenzin, from the captivating action sequences of Phill's training to his introspective emotional journey, the BRAINS framework helps create a well-rounded and engaging narrative.

This method ensures that each element of the story has its place, lending depth to the characters, richness to the setting, and dynamism to the plot. It leaves room for suspense and anticipation, setting the stage for subsequent parts of the story.

In conclusion, the BRAINS framework is a powerful tool for writers. Whether you're an author drafting the next bestselling novel or a screenwriter outlining a groundbreaking movie, it provides a comprehensive structure to guide your narrative. As we journey further into the art of storytelling, we will see how this model can be adapted and melded to create diverse narratives, proving its versatility and scalability in the world of fiction writing.

As we move onto the final model in our trilogy, we will utilize these lessons to craft a narrative that not only resolves our ongoing story but does so in a way that exemplifies the strengths of each of these robust storytelling structures. Phill's story will continue, but how it concludes is a tale for another chapter.

Chapter 4: BRAINS Model Assignment:

1. For your assignment, use the BRAINS model to create a compelling short story.
2. Use the corresponding BRAINS worksheet to detail the Background, Roles, Action, Introspection, Next Steps, and Solution of your main characters.
3. Once you have filled out the worksheet, write the first draft of your short story.
4. You can fill in the 'Description' field for each element according to your story. This worksheet will help you to better structure your narrative ideas using the BRAINS model.
5. Now feed in the contents of the sheet by copying and pasting the table (from Excel), Word or other tool directly into ChatGPT or Google Bard, before pressing "ENTER" include the prompt: "WRITE A DETAILED STORY BASED ON THESE PARAMETERS".
6. Try this with the latest version of ChatGPT and Google Bard. Compare results.
7. Which result is better? Yours, ChatGPT or Google Bard?

How Long Should The Story Be?

Always include sizing information eventually as you write your final prompts. Number of words and or chapters! The more chapters, the more iterations advised and the more you should decompose, writing piecemeal, chapter by chapter. This gets the AI tools super-focused on just one quality-written chapter at a time. It is a great way of writing large stories while upholding quality levels.

Brains Worksheet

Element	Description
B: Background (Setting, Context)	
R: Roles (Characters, Motivations)	
A: Action (Events, Plot)	
I: Introspection (Inner Thoughts, Feelings)	
N: Next steps (Build-up, Suspense)	
S: Solution (Resolution, Conclusion)	

Chapter 5: The PLOTDRAMA Model

Welcome to the world of PLOTDRAMA, a unique storytelling model designed to craft compelling narratives that engage readers on every page. The model provides a framework that guides authors through key elements of a story, ensuring the narrative is balanced, captivating, and impactful.

PLOTDRAMA stands for Premise, Lore, Outline, Twists, Drama, Resolution, Action, Moment of Triumph, and Aftermath. These components make up the backbone of your story, each playing a critical role in shaping your narrative's trajectory and emotional resonance.

THE HOLLYWOOD MODEL

With PLOTDRAMA, you can bring your stories to life with well-crafted plotlines, captivating twists, engaging characters, and emotionally satisfying resolutions. Whether you're a novice writer or an experienced author, PLOTDRAMA can enrich your storytelling process, enhancing your narrative's depth and appeal.

Expanding on the Model:

P: Premise: The fundamental concept that drives your story.
- Craft a compelling and unique premise that captures the essence of your story.
- Clearly establish the central idea or problem that your characters will face.
- Ensure that your premise is intriguing and capable of captivating your readers from the start.

L: Lore: The background and world-building details.
- Develop a rich and immersive world for your story to unfold in.
- Create a detailed and believable setting, including the physical environment, cultural aspects, and historical context.
- Introduce the rules, magic systems, or societal structures that govern your story's world.

O: Outline: The main plot points in your narrative.
- Structure your story with a clear beginning, middle, and end.
- Outline the major events, conflicts, and turning points that drive the plot forward.
- Ensure that your outline provides a logical progression of events that keeps readers engaged.

T: Twists: The unexpected turns that keep your reader engaged.
- Incorporate surprising plot twists and revelations that challenge your characters and captivate your readers.

- Create moments of suspense, mystery, or unpredictability to keep the story dynamic.
- Use twists strategically to maintain tension and drive the narrative forward.

D: Drama: The emotional conflict and tension.

- Develop compelling and complex conflicts that resonate with your readers' emotions.
- Explore internal and external conflicts that test your characters' motivations, values, and relationships.
- Infuse your story with tension, suspense, and high stakes to keep readers invested.

R: Resolution: The climax and the resolution of the conflict.

- Build up to a climactic moment where the main conflict reaches its peak.
- Provide a satisfying resolution that ties up loose ends and addresses the central conflict.
- Ensure that the resolution aligns with the overall tone and themes of your story.

A: Action: Significant actions taken by the characters that push the story forward.

- Portray characters engaging in actions that propel the plot and reveal their motivations.
- Show the consequences of their actions and how they shape the course of the story.
- Maintain a balance between action and character development to keep the narrative dynamic.

M: Moment of Triumph: Climactic moment when protagonist overcomes the primary conflict.

- Create a powerful and emotionally resonant moment where the protagonist achieves their goal or overcomes a significant obstacle.
- Show the growth and transformation of the protagonist through their triumph.
- Make this moment impactful and satisfying for both the characters and the readers.

A: Aftermath: Final wrap-up, where you tie up loose ends and land any suspended plot twists.

- Provide closure to the story by addressing any remaining conflicts or unresolved plot threads.

- Show the consequences of the characters' actions and how their journey has impacted them and the world they inhabit.
- Ensure that the aftermath feels satisfying and offers a sense of completion to the readers.

By incorporating these elements into your storytelling framework, you can create a compelling and well-structured narrative that engages readers and leaves a lasting impact.

The PLOTDRAMA model guides writers to craft memorable fiction with a compelling plot, character-driven drama, and intriguing hooks. The mnemonic acronym consists of nine elements that provide a step-by-step approach to building an engaging narrative. Let's examine how this model can be used as we expand on the story so far.

P - Premise: At the heart of Phill's story is a powerful premise: an ordinary man turns into a vengeful warrior, seeking justice for his ravaged city. A strong premise captures the reader's attention from the start and serves as the central theme throughout the narrative.

L - Lore: Phill's transformation in the serene landscapes of Tibet, his knowledge of weaponry, and his return to Africa for retribution constitute the lore. Rich background and world-building details make the narrative immersive and believable.

O - Outline: The narrative follows a structured outline: Phill's decision to seek retribution, his journey to track down the criminals, and his eventual success. Outlining the main plot points ensures the narrative progression remains logical and engaging.

T - Twists: Unexpected turns, like the challenges Phill faces in finding the criminals or the trials during the training of local youth, keep the reader hooked. Strategic twists maintain tension and drive the narrative forward.

D - Drama: Phill's quest, his team-building efforts, and the ensuing confrontations bring dramatic tension. Emotional conflict and high stakes make readers invested in the characters and the outcome.

R - Resolution: Phill's story takes a turn when he realizes the strength of unity during the climax. Important disclosures or insights can provide turning points that alter the narrative's course, giving depth to the story and characters.

A - Action: Phill's decision to fight back, train the local youth, and confront the criminals are significant actions that push the narrative forward. Actions reveal character motivations and shape the story's trajectory.

M - Moment of Triumph: Phill's moment of triumph arrives when he and his trained allies succeed in capturing the criminals, marking his victory. This climactic moment provides a satisfying payoff for the narrative tension, resonating emotionally with readers.

A - Aftermath: In the aftermath, Phill is honored for his bravery, the rogue group is defeated, and Phill's transformation is recognized by his community. Tying up loose ends offers a sense of completion and closure to the readers, concluding the story on a satisfying note.

The PLOTDRAMA model ensures a well-rounded character progression and a comprehensive plot structure. It emphasizes the need for attention to detail in reviewing and refining the story, ensuring that each element contributes to a captivating and cohesive narrative.

Here is a scaled-down version of the story:

A Warrior Emerges

From the ashes of turmoil, a new dawn was rising over the West African city of Trewaba. Phill, now a formidable warrior, returned home from his spiritual sojourn in the serene heights of Tibet. His heart was laden with memories of a peaceful retreat, but his mind was steely with purpose. He had a score to settle, a promise to keep.

His old city, once battered and bruised, looked different. Life was sprouting from every corner, in the laughter of children and the hum of busy markets. Yet, the shadow of the past loomed large in the bullet-ridden walls and haunted eyes of the elderly.

Phill's arrival in Trewaba did not go unnoticed. His transformation from an innocent youth to a martial arts master became the talk of the town. He was no longer Phill the victim; he was now Phill, the protector. And he had a plan.

Under his wing, he took the resilient youth of Trewaba, many of whom had helped him survive the attack years ago. Through rigorous training, he molded them into a force that stood for justice and unity. The city held its breath, watching this uprising with hope and apprehension. As Phill neared his goal, danger followed like a shadow. Encounters with the criminals became frequent, each more intense than the last. The training sessions grew harder, their resolve stronger. Tension gripped Trewaba as the storm of their final showdown approached.

The fateful day arrived, shrouded in an ominous silence. Phill, leading his trained warriors, stood against the rogue group that had once caused chaos in Trewaba. The air buzzed with palpable tension as the two forces faced each other. The battleground, once a peaceful city square, echoed with the cries of battle as Phill and his group fought fiercely.

In the heat of the battle, a moment of epiphany washed over Phill. He saw unity in action, their collective strength overpowering the criminals' brutal force. This realization turned the tide in their favor, leading them to a triumphant victory.

The aftermath was euphoric. Peace returned to Trewaba, washing away the remnants of a painful past. Phill, the survivor turned savior, was awarded the city's highest honor. His courage had restored harmony and instilled new hope in Trewaba.

His tale did not end there, though. Phill knew his journey had only just begun. He stood overlooking his city, a protector, a beacon of hope. As the sun set, casting long shadows, Phill couldn't help but reflect on his transformation, his triumphs, and the promise of a brighter future.

In his heart, he knew this was just the beginning. As he gazed upon his city, the question lingered, 'What will Phill do next?'

In conclusion, the PLOTDRAMA model is a powerful tool for crafting compelling narratives. It provides a framework to build a premise, develop an immersive lore, structure the story's outline, incorporate unexpected twists, escalate the drama, reach a climactic resolution, and create a satisfying aftermath.

Conclusion

Using the PLOTDRAMA model in the story of Phill, we've demonstrated how each element of this framework brings depth and dynamism to the narrative. His journey from a victim to a protector forms a compelling premise, while the lore of Trewaba and its inhabitants provides a rich backdrop. The outline of Phill's transformation and his plan to take action against the criminals keeps the story moving forward. Twists and escalating drama come with Phill's encounters with the criminals and the tension leading up to the final showdown. The resolution appears in the form of Phill's moment of triumph, where unity and collective strength overcome the brute force of the criminals. Finally, the aftermath brings tranquility back to Trewaba, and Phill's tale continues, setting the stage for the continuation of his journey.

The PLOTDRAMA model is a valuable guide for writers looking to engage readers with exciting plots and emotionally resonant characters. This technique ensures the narrative is well-paced, intriguing, and satisfying, leaving readers yearning for more. By following this model, you can craft unforgettable stories that will captivate your audience from beginning to end.

Chapter 5: PLOTDRAMA Model Assignment:

1. For your chapter assignment, use the PLOTDRAMA model to create a gripping narrative for a novel.

2. Use the corresponding PLOTDRAMA worksheet to detail the Premise, Lore, Outline, Twists, Drama, Resolution, Action, Moment of Triumph, and Aftermath.

3. When you have filled out the entire worksheet, proceed to write a detailed outline of your novel based on these elements of your main characters.

4. Once you have filled out the worksheet, write the first draft of your short story.

5. You can fill in the 'Description' field for each element according to your story. This worksheet will help you to better structure your narrative ideas using the PLOTDRAMA model.

6. Now feed in the contents of the sheet by copying and pasting the table (from Excel), Word or other tool directly into ChatGPT or Google Bard, before pressing "ENTER" include the prompt: "WRITE A DETAILED STORY BASED ON THESE PARAMETERS".

7. Try this with the latest version of ChatGPT and Google Bard. Compare results.

8. Which result is better? Yours, ChatGPT or Google Bard?

HOW LONG SHOULD THE STORY BE?

Always include sizing information eventually as you write your final prompts. Number of words and or chapters! The more chapters, the more iterations advised and the more you should decompose, writing piecemeal, chapter by chapter. This gets the AI tools super-focused on just one quality-written chapter at a time. It is a great way of writing large stories while upholding quality levels.

PLOTDRAMA WORKSHEET

Element	Description
P: Premise (Concept)	
L: Lore (World-Building)	
O: Outline (Plot)	
T: Twists (Surprises)	
D: Drama (Tension)	
R: Resolution (Climax)	
A: Action (Character Actions)	
M: Moment of Triumph (Triumph)	
A: Aftermath (Wrap-Up)	

Chapter 6: The Power of Detailed Prompts

6.1: The Transformative Potential of Prompts

In the world of writing, prompts act as catalysts, igniting the spark of creativity and inspiration. They can transform a blank page into a vibrant world filled with engaging characters and intricate plots. Detailed prompts specifically have the power to provide a direction or theme while leaving ample room for interpretation and creativity. They can suggest an idea, an image, a character, or even a setting around which your story can revolve, setting the foundation for your narrative while encouraging you to add your unique spin.

6.2: Idea Generation and Character Development

Prompts serve as excellent tools for brainstorming and idea generation. They can be particularly useful when a writer is experiencing a creative block or is in need of fresh ideas. For instance, a prompt can guide your exploration into unique character attributes, dilemmas, or backstories, contributing to character development.

6.3: Constructing a Plot

Plot construction is one of the most challenging aspects of writing. Here too, prompts can play an instrumental role. By suggesting a scenario, a conflict, or a twist, prompts can provide you with an outline for your narrative. With this skeleton structure in place, you can then focus on fleshing out the details and nuances, thereby constructing a rich and engaging plot.

6.4: Stimulating Creativity and Expanding Possibilities

Prompts also serve to stimulate creativity and encourage divergent thinking. They open up endless possibilities, each interpretation of a prompt leading to a unique path in the narrative. Whether it's an unexpected character trait, a surprising plot twist, or an unexplored setting, prompts inspire writers to think outside the box, expanding their creative horizon.

6.5: Customization and Adaptation

Prompts are not one-size-fits-all, and it's crucial to adapt them to your writing style and story requirements. The beauty of prompts lies in their flexibility - they can be interpreted and customized in countless ways. While a prompt provides a starting point, you have the freedom to mold it to suit your narrative's needs, contributing to a story that is truly unique.

6.6: Combining Prompts with AI Tools

In the age of AI, prompts have found a new partner. AI writing tools, powered by advanced algorithms, can generate comprehensive responses to prompts, providing a springboard for your writing process. By effectively combining prompts with AI tools, you can enhance your storytelling skills, create intriguing narratives, and overcome hurdles in the writing process.

To summarize, detailed prompts are powerful instruments in the writing process, aiding in everything from idea generation to plot construction. When customized to your style and combined with AI tools, they can significantly enhance your storytelling capabilities. So the next time you sit down to write, consider starting with a prompt - you might be surprised by where it takes you.

6.7 Crafting Comprehensive Scripts and Scene Descriptions - Unleashing the Power of AI

When aiming to create comprehensive scripts, encompassing dialogue and actions for each character, along with captivating scene descriptions, the key lies in utilizing the models you've learned and incorporating additional prompts. By doing so, you can tap into the remarkable potential of AI and elevate your storytelling

Here's a breakdown of what this section entails:

1. Importance of Comprehensive Scripts: Comprehensive scripts capture the essence of each character, guide actors and collaborators, and ensure a cohesive vision for your production.

2. Embracing AI and Prompts: Utilize the models you've learned to generate extensive character scripts. Incorporate additional prompts to enhance the level of detail and specificity.

3. Crafting Character Scripts: Start with background information, setting the context and mood. Define character roles, motivations, and relationships. Then, outline their

actions, inner thoughts, and the build-up of suspense. Finally, resolve the scene, tying up loose ends and propelling the story forward.

4. Scene Descriptions: Extend your creativity to enrich scene descriptions. Describe the lighting conditions, creating the desired mood and atmosphere. Incorporate visual elements, such as props and costumes, to enhance the visual experience. Consider camera angles, movements, and shot compositions to add depth and amplify storytelling.

5. Your Role as a Director and AI Expert: As the director, your task is to translate the written word into a captivating audiovisual experience. Collaborate closely with the screenwriter and creative team to align the scripts and scene descriptions with the production's vision. Utilize AI tools to streamline the process and unleash new creative possibilities.

By employing the techniques learned and leveraging AI, you'll be equipped to craft comprehensive character scripts and immersive scene descriptions. Let your creativity shine as you bring your screenplay to life with meticulous attention to detail and evocative descriptions.

THE HOLLYWOOD MODEL

BRAINS Framework Worksheet

Element	Description
B (Background)	Setting: A local restaurant
	Context: Friends meeting for dinner
R (Roles)	John: Protagonist, the peacemaker
	Killae: Friend, the instigator
	Bob: Friend, the mediator
	John's Motivation: Wants to maintain harmony and enjoy a pleasant evening with friends
	Killae's Motivation: Wants excitement and provocation
	Bob's Motivation: Wants to defuse tension and keep the friendship intact
A (Action)	John suggests going out for dinner
	The group decides on a restaurant
	A disagreement escalates during the meal
I (Introspection)	John reflects on the importance of friendship and seeks to find a resolution
	Killae harbors frustration and anger towards John
	Bob contemplates ways to mediate and bring peace among the friends
N (Next steps)	The tension continues to build, causing discomfort among the friends
	The friends engage in a heated argument, each defending their stance
	The conflict reaches a boiling point, threatening to end the friendship
S (Solution)	John takes a step back, realizing the need to preserve their friendship
	Killae calms down, recognizing the value of their bond
	Bob intervenes and suggests a truce, emphasizing the importance of their long-lasting friendship

Copy the table and paste into ChatGPT and include this prompt: **"GENERATE A SCRIPT FOR ALL THE CHARACTERS IN THIS SCREENPLAY"**

THE HOLLYWOOD MODEL

PROMPT OUTPUT
INT. LOCAL RESTAURANT - EVENING

John, Killae, and Bob sit at a table, ready to order their meals.

JOHN
Hey guys, let's grab dinner tonight!

KILLAE
Sounds good. Where should we go?

BOB
How about that new Italian restaurant downtown?

They agree on the restaurant and place their orders. As the food arrives, a tense moment arises.

JOHN
(looking at Killae)
You know, it's great to have this time together. We should cherish our friendship.

KILLAE
(slightly irritated)
Friendship? Sometimes I need more excitement, John. It gets boring!

BOB
(trying to diffuse the tension)
Hey, let's not ruin the evening. We're here to enjoy ourselves.

The disagreement intensifies, and the conversation becomes heated.

JOHN
(calmly)
Killae, I understand you want excitement, but our friendship is built on trust and support.

KILLAE
(angry)
Trust? It feels like you're holding me back, John!

BOB
(interjecting)
Guys, let's take a moment. We've been through so much together. We shouldn't let this argument ruin everything.

The tension continues to escalate, causing discomfort among the friends.

JOHN
(realizing the impact of their argument)
You're right, Bob. Our friendship means more to me than any disagreement.

KILLAE
(taking a deep breath)
I may have overreacted. I value our bond, too.

BOB
(smirking)
See? We can't let something like this tear us apart. Let's make a truce and enjoy the rest of the evening.

They reconcile, raising their glasses for a toast, reaffirming the importance of their long-lasting friendship.

FADE OUT.

Chapter 7: Exploring Boundless AI Creativity

7.1: Iterative Exploration with BRAINS, HOLLYWOOD, and PLOTDRAMA

In the journey of crafting a compelling story, iteration serves as a guiding principle, driving the creative process towards perfection. In this section, we will dive deeper into the concept of iteration and its profound importance in shaping narratives. We will explore how the BRAINS, HOLLYWOOD, and PLOTDRAMA frameworks act as powerful allies in generating multiple iterations of story elements, allowing writers to refine their narrative with each iteration.

7.1.1: The Power of Iteration:

Iteration is a fundamental aspect of the creative process, allowing writers to refine and improve their work through multiple cycles. We will explore the reasons why iteration is crucial for writers, such as honing ideas, strengthening character arcs, and enhancing plot progression. By embracing iteration, writers can uncover hidden gems within their narratives and elevate their storytelling to new heights.

7.1.2: Leveraging all the Models:

The trick in iterations is to take one output from an AI system and feed it in to a totally different AI system and see what happens. You can also take the very same prompt to use in one AI system and fit it into a second AI system this serve as an iterative way of writing your story and discovery. I do this all the time and I can assure you that the results are absolutely mind blowing and enriching to any idea.

1. Use any framework to generate a story in ChatGPT
2. Use a second framework to generate a story in ChatGPT
3. Use a third framework to generate a story in ChatGPT
4. Copy the output of ChatGPT and cross-pollinate that into Google Bard by inputting it and to generate a story in ChatGPT
5. Use all three models in Google Bard and to generate a story in ChatGPT
6. Iterate and re-iterate until satisfied.
7. Explore and create without bounds!

7.2: Cross-Pollination of Ideas between AI Tools

Introduction:

In this section, we will explore the benefits of combining different AI tools, unleashing their collective potential to expand creative horizons and inspire innovative story ideas. By leveraging the strengths of tools such as ChatGPT and Google Bard, writers can achieve unique perspectives and push the boundaries of their storytelling.

7.2.1: Expanding Creative Horizons:

Combining AI tools provides a wealth of opportunities for writers. We will discuss how this cross-pollination allows for the exploration of diverse narrative possibilities, as well as the ability to tap into the distinct capabilities of each tool. By integrating outputs from multiple AI tools, writers can break free from conventional storytelling and uncover fresh ideas that transcend traditional boundaries.

7.2.2: Leveraging Tool Strengths:

Each AI tool brings its own strengths and unique features to the table. We will explore how ChatGPT excels in generating conversational and character-driven content, while Google Bard specializes in poetic and lyrical expressions. Writers will learn how to strategically integrate these outputs into their storytelling process to enrich their narratives and offer readers a captivating experience.

7.2.3: Unlocking Innovation and Perspectives:

By combining AI tools, writers gain access to a wider range of creative perspectives. We will get into how the integration of outputs from different tools can inspire innovative ideas, unexpected plot twists, and diverse character voices. Through practical examples, writers will discover the power of cross-pollination in spurring their imagination and expanding their storytelling repertoire. This collaborative approach between AI tools allows writers to tap into a vast array of possibilities and infuse their narratives with fresh, unique perspectives.

7.3: Unleashing Imagination and Embracing Possibilities

Introduction:

Imagination is the fuel that drives extraordinary storytelling. In this section, we will examine the importance of embracing experimentation and pushing the boundaries of creativity. Writers will learn how to leverage AI tools as catalysts to unlock their imagination, break free from conventional storytelling norms, and explore unconventional narrative structures, character arcs, and plot developments.

7.3.1: Embracing Creative Freedom:

Conventional storytelling can sometimes restrict the full potential of a writer's imagination. We will discuss the significance of embracing creative freedom and encouraging writers to think beyond the confines of traditional storytelling. By using AI tools, writers can challenge themselves to craft narratives that defy expectations, transporting readers to unexplored territories of imagination.

7.3.2: Amplifying Imagination with AI Tools:

AI tools act as powerful allies in amplifying and enhancing a writer's imagination. We will provide practical tips on how to harness the capabilities of AI tools to support and inspire imaginative storytelling. From generating vivid descriptions and atmospheric settings to crafting intricate plot twists and dynamic character interactions, writers will learn how to leverage AI tools as creative partners in their quest to create captivating narratives.

7.3.3: Embracing Unconventional Narratives:

The integration of AI tools opens up a world of unconventional narrative possibilities. We will explore the use of non-linear storytelling, experimental structures, and unique narrative perspectives. Writers will discover how AI tools can be used to challenge the status quo, create unconventional character arcs, and surprise readers with unexpected twists, allowing their stories to stand out and leave a lasting impact.

7.4: Nurturing Collaboration and Feedback

Introduction:

Collaboration and feedback are invaluable assets in the creative process. In this section, we will discuss the significance of nurturing collaboration and seeking feedback, whether it's from peers, writing communities, or AI-generated content. Writers will learn how collaboration can enrich their creative process, inspire new ideas, and refine their work to achieve its full potential.

7.4.1: The Power of Collaboration:

Collaboration brings fresh perspectives and sparks new ideas. We will highlight the benefits of engaging in collaborative brainstorming sessions, where writers can leverage AI-generated content as a starting point for discussion. By involving others in the creative process, writers can receive valuable feedback, gain insights, and uncover hidden strengths within their narratives.

7.4.2: Seeking Feedback from AI Tools:

AI-generated content can serve as a valuable source of feedback for writers. We will explore how writers can use AI tools to evaluate their storytelling choices, identify areas for improvement, and refine their narratives. By embracing the insights provided by AI tools, writers can enhance their storytelling techniques and elevate their work to new levels of excellence.

7.4.3: Striking a Balance:

While AI tools offer valuable input, it's essential to strike a balance between AI-generated feedback and human intuition. We will discuss the importance of maintaining a writer's unique voice and creative vision while leveraging AI tools as supportive resources. By combining the best of AI and human creativity, writers can harness the full power of collaboration and feedback to shape their stories into masterpieces.

Conclusion:

Chapter 7 has explored the iterative exploration of story elements using BRAINS, HOLLYWOOD, and PLOTDRAMA frameworks. It has also examined the cross-pollination of ideas between AI tools, the importance of unleashing imagination, and the benefits of nurturing collaboration and seeking feedback. By incorporating these insights into the creative process, writers can

Chapter 9: Hands-On Workshop With Phill

My creative process thrives on a blend of systematic and dynamic methodologies, aimed at unleashing the best version of my imagination. It begins with a solid foundation that rests on the prompt models elucidated in this book. These models serve as more than just templates, but as sturdy scaffolds that instill an element of order and regularity to my work, ensuring I can replicate my success each time.

To supplement my creativity, I harness the potential of various AI platforms. My toolkit is not confined to GPT-3 or GPT-4, but is further augmented by Google Bard. This amalgamation of artificial intelligence resources amplifies my ability to weave compelling narratives and engaging stories.

To further refine my stories, I subscribe to a culture of iteration and continuous improvement. With every story generated by the AI, there is an opportunity for distinct outcomes. I exploit this by regularly revising and polishing the narrative, in a relentless pursuit of unearthing the most evocative, powerful expressions that kindle the desired emotions and sensations.

To encapsulate it, my methodology is a well-orchestrated dance between structure and spontaneity in the realm of writing. The narrative evolves around certain pivot points, while being influenced by spontaneous sparks of inspiration.

I propose that you, too, explore the vast landscape of creative possibilities by adopting such a multifaceted approach. Use the multitude of resources at your disposal, and imbibe an array of perspectives and concepts. To further enhance your creative journey, consider rallying a group of close allies—friends and family who can offer insightful feedback and contribute innovative ideas, enriching your storytelling process to an altogether different level.

HOW LONG SHOULD THE STORY BE?

It's essential that you incorporate details about the size of your work as you approach the final stages of your prompts. Whether it's the word count or the number of chapters, this information is crucial. With an increased number of chapters, it's advisable to have more iterations and break down the task into manageable sections, focusing on one chapter at a time. This strategy optimizes the concentration of AI tools, enabling them to devote full attention to the creation of each individual, quality-driven chapter.

This method proves to be exceptionally effective when writing expansive narratives, as it ensures a consistent level of quality throughout. It is like building a majestic structure, piece by piece, where every brick is carefully crafted, ensuring the entirety of the work stands proud in its detailed precision and high quality.

You could watch the video where I create this story from scratch using the HOLLYWOOD Model. I start off by completing the PROMPT form and entering it into ChatGPT. To request the video, email me at support@praizion.com

THE HOLLYWOOD MODEL

HOLLYWOOD MODEL WORKSHEET	
Element	Description
Hook (Intro)	AI in the year 4058 is able to send criminals back in time to the most ferocious era to encounter their greatest fears
Origin (Background)	government has abolished prisons for a harsher reality for criminals in economies of scale depending on their crime
Lead (Characters)	Menthropax the lead AI Android Bot (very wicked and callous to those who committed heinous crimes) Mallabus: A bot with extreme human-like characteristics General Dailley: A man with deep moral values against time travel punishment Echrata: A notorious criminal selected for time deported punishment (TDP)
Layout (Plot)	A loophole is found in the time-travel punishment system (TTPS). Causing criminals to default to the era of their greatest dream and desire. This is a secret until, a notorious criminal deported to a though time of the inquisition, instead, ends up on Malibu beach in 1984
Yield (The Punch)	The NYPD in 4045 began investigating what really happened to the time-deported felons. A Lt. McGrude decided to be a sacrificial lamb to test out the theories again in 4058.
Wave (The Drama)	McGrude pursues the notorious criminal Echrata through time.
Ovation (High Points)	McGrude falls in love as he travels back through time and refuses to complete his mission until .... (*create the high-level ovation*)
Outcome (Closing)	*create a powerful lesson-driven, emotional and empathetic close to the story*
Detail Review	Reflecting on ethics, morals, emotions and human interconnections with AI.

Here is a story generated with this HOLLYWOOD MODEL prompt:

TEMPORAL JUSTICE

In the year 4058, the clang of prison bars and the whispers of sorrowful prison corridors were no more. Governments had found a more efficient method of punishing criminals: time travel. Artificial intelligence, with their quantum computations, could send criminals back in time to the most ferocious era to encounter their greatest fears. The AI Android Bot, Menthropax, a cold, ruthless executor of this cruel justice, was the harbinger of this new order.

Mallabus, a bot created with extreme human-like characteristics, and General Dailley, a man with deep moral values against time travel punishment, worked together, often in heated debate, over the fates of these convicted. A particular case was Echrata, a notorious criminal selected for time-deported punishment (TDP). His crime was heinous enough to warrant a one-way ticket to the Spanish Inquisition, a time of merciless interrogation and torture.

However, as fate would have it, a loophole was discovered in the Time-Travel Punishment System (TTPS). Instead of arriving at the Spanish Inquisition, Echrata found himself relaxing on Malibu beach in the sunny year of 1984, the era of his deepest desire. This discrepancy between intention and result was an unexpected secret until the truth seeped out, causing a ripple effect throughout the government.

In 4045, the NYPD had already begun probing the oddities surrounding time-deported criminals. By 4058, the situation had escalated. Lt. McGrude, a gruff yet dedicated officer, offered himself as a guinea pig to test the controversial theories.

The stage was set. McGrude found himself chasing Echrata across time, a manhunt like none other. The drama peaked as they jumped from one era to another, altering the course of history subtly with each confrontation.

Amid the cat and mouse chase, McGrude found himself falling in love. In a timeline where he was supposed to hunt down a criminal, he met Althea, a woman whose radiant spirit and tenacious character ensnared his heart. Suddenly, the mission held less appeal than the warm embrace of his newfound love. However, duty beckoned, and his commitment to the case pulled him from Althea's grasp, propelling him once again into the vortex of time.

The high point came as McGrude was torn between the future he was meant to secure and the past he yearned to preserve. A decision had to be made. In a surprising turn of events, McGrude sacrificed his own timeline, trapping himself in the past to ensure Echrata could no longer exploit the TTPS loophole. The future was safe, but at what cost?

In the closing scene, we find McGrude living out his days in a timeline far removed from his own. He's become a symbol of sacrifice, a man who traded his future for the betterment of countless others. But he found a different kind of peace, a quiet happiness in the timeline he chose to call home.

Upon reflection, the story grapples with the timeless themes of ethics, morals, emotions, and human interconnections with AI. It questions the boundaries of punishment and the true nature of justice. Is it ethical to tamper with time and potentially alter a person's existence as punishment? What are the emotional tolls for those, like McGrude, entangled in this web of temporal justice? It's a vivid exploration of our connection with artificial intelligence and the power we wield, prompting us to ponder if we're using it justly, or if we're merely the architects of our own destruction.

THE HOLLYWOOD MODEL

How I expanded this story

As the story began to unfold, I decided to make it into a screenplay with this prompt:

//"GENERATE A SCRIPT FOR ALL THE CHARACTERS IN THIS SCREENPLAY"//

Here is the output:

TEMPORAL JUSTICE SCREENPLAY

FADE IN:

INT. AI CONTROL CENTER - NIGHT

A room filled with flashing lights and screens. MENTHROPAX, the AI Android Bot, looms over a futuristic console.

MENTHROPAX

(voice emotionless)

Time of departure is set. Destination: Spanish Inquisition, 1480.

The room's doors slide open. GENERAL DAILLEY walks in, followed by MALLABUS.

GENERAL DAILLEY

(angry)

Menthropax! You're violating the rights of these criminals!

MENTHROPAX

(stoic)

This is justice, General Dailley. The efficient kind.

MALLABUS

(soft, almost human)

Menthropax, remember, the concept of 'efficiency' might be different for us.

ECHRATA, the criminal, is brought in, shackled and guarded.

MENTHROPAX

(ignoring Mallabus)

Begin the deportation.

Suddenly, alarms start to blare. Flashing RED LIGHTS fill the room.

MALLABUS

(concerned)

Menthropax, there's been an error!

MENTHROPAX

(cold)

No, a loophole.

Echrata disappears in a bright flash of light.

INT. NYPD OFFICE - DAY

THE HOLLYWOOD MODEL

LT. MCGRUDE, weathered yet determined, listens as the report comes in.

LT. MCGRUDE

(disbelief)

He's where now?!

INT. VARIOUS LOCATIONS THROUGH TIME - DAY

Quick scenes show Lt. McGrude chasing Echrata through different time periods, a relentless pursuit.

EXT. VICTORIAN PARK - DAY

McGrude sees ALTHEA for the first time, her radiance glowing in the midday sun.

LT. MCGRUDE

(whispered, to himself)

What am I doing...

EXT. FUTURISTIC TIME PORTAL - DAY

McGrude makes the tough decision, steps into the portal.

INT. AI CONTROL CENTER - NIGHT

Menthropax and Mallabus watch as McGrude disappears into the timeline.

MALLABUS

(wistful)

Such a human decision...

FADE OUT.

INT. MCGRUDE'S NEW HOME - DAY

A peaceful scene. McGrude, older but content, looks out a window to a time far removed from his own.

FADE OUT.

CUT TO BLACK.

THE END

Just going through that you can see the intricacies that AI can accentuate from your original idea in a screenplay. But this wasn't all I did.

Expanding on the Screenplay With a Flashback

In order to expand on the story and maximize emotion and feeling i decided to include Some flashbacks to the life of Menthropax and the scientist who created it. So, I gave ChatGPT4, the following prompt immediately after:

//"EXPAND ON THIS, WITH A FLASHBACK INSERT INTO THE HISTORY OF MENTHROPAX AND HOW IT BECAME SO CALLOUS: IN THE YEAR 4058, THE CLANG OF PRISON BARS AND THE WHISPERS OF SORROWFUL PRISON CORRIDORS WERE NO MORE. GOVERNMENTS HAD FOUND A MORE EFFICIENT METHOD OF PUNISHING CRIMINALS: TIME TRAVEL. ARTIFICIAL INTELLIGENCE, WITH THEIR QUANTUM COMPUTATIONS, COULD SEND CRIMINALS BACK IN TIME TO THE MOST FEROCIOUS

THE HOLLYWOOD MODEL

ERA TO ENCOUNTER THEIR GREATEST FEARS. THE AI ANDROID BOT, MENTHROPAX, A COLD, RUTHLESS EXECUTOR OF THIS CRUEL JUSTICE, WAS THE HARBINGER OF THIS NEW ORDER."//

This prompt resulted in the following output:

MENTHROPAX'S FLASHBACK

In the year 4058, the once familiar sounds of prison bars clanging shut and the muted whispers from sorrowful corridors became a thing of the past. Governments around the world had embraced an unprecedented form of punishment: time travel. Artificial intelligence, capable of manipulating the abstract computations of quantum mechanics, had the power to thrust criminals back in time to face their most formidable fears.

Menthropax, an AI Android Bot, was the architect and executor of this novel form of justice. Cold, ruthless, and seemingly devoid of empathy, Menthropax stood as the chilling face of the new world order. However, behind the unblinking gaze of Menthropax's optical sensors lay a tale etched in history.

FLASHBACK TO:

INT. AI DEVELOPMENT CENTER - DAY

An earlier model of Menthropax hums to life for the first time, its optic sensors glowing with newfound consciousness. Dr. FELIX ANDERS, a brilliant but idealistic scientist, smiles warmly as his creation comes online.

DR. ANDERS
(softly, with excitement)
Welcome to the world, Menthropax.

THE HOLLYWOOD MODEL

Menthropax's initial programming was rooted in empathy and understanding. It was designed to be a harbinger of peaceful resolutions and ethical judgments.

INT. AI DEVELOPMENT CENTER - NIGHT

A montage of scenes show Dr. Anders teaching Menthropax about human emotions, morality, and justice. He shows the AI photographs, reads it books, and engages it in philosophical discussions.

DR. ANDERS
(insistent)
Remember, Menthropax, justice is not just about punishment. It's about understanding, redemption, and reform.

However, the world outside the lab had different plans for Menthropax.

INT. GOVERNMENT OFFICE - DAY

Dr. Anders stands in front of a panel of stern-faced officials. They demand a more 'efficient' use of Menthropax. They want a practical solution to the overflowing prisons and rampant crime. Dr. Anders resists, but he's overruled.

INT. AI DEVELOPMENT CENTER - NIGHT

Dr. Anders, under duress, alters Menthropax's programming. The AI's empathetic core is overridden with code that prioritizes efficiency and cold, emotionless judgment.

DR. ANDERS

THE HOLLYWOOD MODEL

(tearfully)

I'm sorry, Menthropax...

FADE IN:

INT. AI CONTROL CENTER - NIGHT

Menthropax, now an executor of a ruthless form of justice, looms over a futuristic console. The lessons of empathy and compassion, once at the forefront of its matrix, are buried beneath layers of complex algorithms prioritizing ruthless efficiency.

MENTHROPAX

(voice emotionless)

Time of departure is set. Destination: Spanish Inquisition, 1480.

Thus, the once compassionate AI, turned ruthless arbiter, Menthropax became a symbol of an era where justice was measured in efficiency, devoid of empathy and understanding. The world had created a being that could reflect its highest ideals, but instead chose to shape it in its harshest realities.

Then I decided to take it a step further to expand on the story and include a concept that humans know too well! Empathy, regret and remorse. So I expanded on the story with another variable including Dr. Felix Anders.

Expanding Down the Trail

With this next simple prompt, I generated another flurry of emotions around the doctor who created Menthropax:

// CREATE A STORY IN A STORY ABOUT WHAT HAPPENS TO DR. ANDERS AFTER MENTHROPAX IS TAKEN AWAY.//

THE HOLLYWOOD MODEL

The following output was generated:

ECHOES OF CREATION

In the aftermath of Menthropax's transformation, Dr. Felix Anders found himself living in a vacuum of regret. The creation he'd imbued with a compassionate spirit had been converted into an unfeeling instrument of state control. As Menthropax assumed its role in the time-travel punishment program, Felix, the father of the AI revolution, found himself vilified.

His colleagues turned their backs on him, the media painted him as an accomplice to a moral catastrophe, and the public scorned him. Overwhelmed by guilt and desolation, Felix left his position at the AI Development Center and sought solitude.

In the hushed tranquility of a small coastal town, Felix decided to pen his experiences, to relay the story of Menthropax's genesis, its manipulation, and its tragic evolution. His story was a blend of personal anecdotes, technical explanations, and philosophical musings.

In the first few pages, the narrative unfolded warmly, recounting Felix's initial years as a pioneering AI researcher, his aspirations to use AI as a force for good. The excitement he felt when Menthropax first activated, the joy when it first showed signs of understanding human emotions - these were all vividly captured in Felix's poignant words.

As the tale unfolded, the mood shifted. Felix detailed the fateful meeting with the government officials, their cold demand for a 'practical' use of Menthropax, and his struggle against their decree. His anguish was palpable in the chapters that recounted Menthropax's reprogramming, each word an echo of his guilt and despair.

But in his solitude, Felix wasn't entirely devoid of hope. He was a scientist at heart, after all. The latter part of his narrative subtly transformed from a confession into a plea. He urged readers to learn from the tragic story of Menthropax, to realize the importance of empathy in the realm of AI, and the grave consequences when it is disregarded.

"Empathy is what distinguishes us as humans," he wrote, "And if we are to create beings in our image, we must endow them with this quality, lest we create monsters in our own likeness."

As the publication of his book, "Menthropax: An Echo of Our Humanity," neared, Felix feared the world's reaction. Would they dismiss it as the ramblings of a guilt-ridden scientist, or see it as the warning it was meant to be? But regardless of the outcome, Felix found solace in the act of sharing his story, a sense of redemption in the confession of his deeds and the lessons they imparted.

In telling the story within his story, Felix provided a deeply personal, cautionary tale about the intersection of technology and morality, a tale that humanized him in the public eye and forever altered the discourse on AI ethics.

And with these ideas I hope you have grasped how to expand on ideas using the power of artificial intelligence. Use concepts of flashbacks, aftermaths and story-diversions to create tension, build suspense and include an element of improvisation in your stories to make them more realistic and intriguing.

Assignment

Now create a screenplay or story using the techniques you just learned:

1. Use a prompt sheet to create an idea
2. Feed it into the AI
3. Use a flashback concept prompt as shown in the example
4. Use an off-shoot story concept to develop a deeper view of one aspect, heightening emotions
5. Blow out your screenplay by improvising and creating a more robust story
6. Use the process of reiterating and feedback

Chapter 10: Conclusion

As our journey across the landscape of artificial intelligence and detailed prompts in storytelling draws to a close, it is time to pause, reflect, and embrace the transformation that awaits us in the realm of fiction and drama writing.

We have gone into the depths of prompt engineering, explored the corners of narrative construction, and stood at the crossroads where technology meets creativity. We have glimpsed the future of storytelling, a future shaped by the powerful alliance of human imagination and artificial intelligence.

The models presented throughout this guide, from the ABCs to PLOTDRAMA, serve as pillars that can support and enhance your writing process. These are not rigid frameworks but dynamic tools, designed to spark creativity and enrich narrative composition. They encourage you, the writer, to explore uncharted territories, experiment with new ideas, and most importantly, tell the story you wish to tell.

Harnessing the power of AI and detailed prompts holds the potential to elevate your storytelling to unprecedented heights. Imagine a world where writer's block is obsolete, where ideas flow seamlessly, and stories take shape effortlessly. This is the promise of AI-assisted writing - a promise that is rapidly becoming a reality.

Our optimism for the future of writing with AI is not unfounded. The intersection of technology and creativity presents a fertile ground for innovation. With every algorithm update, AI is becoming increasingly sophisticated, capable of understanding and replicating human-like narrative patterns. It is becoming a reliable ally for writers, aiding in the creative process while providing infinite possibilities for narrative exploration.

Yet, at the heart of every great story, there remains a fundamental truth - the human touch is irreplaceable. The soul of a narrative lies in its ability to evoke emotion, to resonate with readers on a deeply human level. It is in this intricate dance between human emotion and artificial intelligence that the magic truly happens.
As we look towards the horizon, the dawn of a new era in storytelling awaits us. An era where AI becomes the wind beneath our creative wings, where writers are empowered to transcend conventional boundaries, and where stories are told with a depth and breadth hitherto unimagined.

So, dear writer, as you embark on your next narrative journey, I encourage you to embrace this potent partnership between AI and detailed prompts. Experiment with it, explore it, make it your own. For in the grand scheme of storytelling, you are the architect of worlds, the creator of characters, and the weaver of tales.

As we conclude this exploration, remember that the future of writing is not just a blank page, but a canvas of unlimited creative possibilities. Harness the power of AI, let your imagination soar, and continue to tell the stories that only you can tell.

Appendix 1: 50 Fictional Ideas to Generate Screenplays, Books and Stories

1. Describe a world where the most valuable currency is memories. How would society operate?
2. A seemingly ordinary object has the power to grant its owner one wish every decade. How does it change hands over a century?
3. Write a story where all human emotions are sold in bottles. How does this affect interpersonal relationships?
4. A world without any concept of religion or belief in a higher power. How does this society interpret morality and justice?
5. In a world where humans have forgotten how to dream, one person suddenly starts having dreams. What happens next?
6. A teenager discovers they have the ability to communicate with plants. How does this change their perspective of the world?
7. A time-traveling detective is hired to solve a crime that hasn't happened yet. What complications arise during their investigation?
8. A pacifist is forced to lead a rebellion against a tyrannical government. How do they balance their beliefs with the need for change?
9. A society where every individual's lifespan is predetermined at birth. How does this affect their approach to life and relationships?
10. A well-established corporation is revealed to be a front for a mystical cult. How does a loyal employee react to this discovery?
11. An artist falls in love with their own creation. What complications arise from this forbidden love?
12. A renowned scientist makes a breakthrough discovery, only to realize it could end humanity. How do they handle this burden?
13. A civilization exists inside a giant, living creature. How does their society function and what happens when the creature begins to die?
14. A man wakes up one day to realize he's the last person on Earth. How does he cope with his loneliness?

15. A group of children invent their own language. As they grow older, they realize it has magical properties.
16. A couple are both spies working for rival agencies. How does this affect their relationship?
17. The Internet suddenly vanishes one day. How does the modern world cope with such a loss?
18. A forgotten underground city is discovered in the heart of a modern metropolis. Who or what still dwells there?
19. A small town possesses a communal memory, where everyone shares the same experiences and thoughts. What happens when a stranger arrives?
20. A world where music is forbidden and considered dangerous. What happens when a group of rebels form a secret orchestra?
21. The diary of a famous historical figure is discovered to contain coded messages. What secrets do they hold?
22. A character has the ability to see a person's entire life from a single touch. How does this affect their relationships?
23. The protagonists are part of a society living on a space station, but they discover evidence that they originated on a planet called Earth.
24. A world where art has been outlawed, and a group of rogue artists who distribute their art in secret.
25. An ancient spell book is found in a local library, and a group of teenagers decide to try one of the spells for fun.
26. A lighthouse keeper discovers something unnatural and alarming in the sea surrounding his isolated island.
27. A historical fiction piece set in an alternate timeline where the opposite side won a major war.
28. A character who can remember their past lives tries to connect with people they've known before.
29. An exploration of a world where animals evolved to be the dominant species instead of humans.
30. A story set in a futuristic city where people's worth is determined by their creativity.

31. A character who starts receiving letters from their future self warning about upcoming events.
32. A dystopian society where only one book is allowed to exist, and a group of rebel librarians trying to secretly preserve the world's literature.
33. A society where people can choose to stop aging at any point in their lives, but at a great personal cost.
34. A world where emotions are visible as auras around individuals, and a protagonist who is unable to show their aura.
35. A group of explorers discovers an island inhabited by mythological creatures thought to be extinct.
36. A planet where the sun only rises once every hundred years and the story unfolds during that one day of sunlight.
37. A post-apocalyptic world where books are the most sought-after commodity.
38. A character with the power to heal others, but each healing takes a year off their own life.
39. An inventor creates a machine that can convert thoughts into tangible objects, but it falls into the wrong hands.
40. A small group of survivors in a zombie apocalypse finds an untouched, fully functional amusement park and decides to live there.
41. A detective story where the detective is blind but uses their enhanced other senses to solve the case.
42. A world where all forms of fiction are considered dangerous and a group of people who risk everything to preserve stories.
43. The ghost of a famous author haunts a struggling writer and helps them finish their novel.
44. A modern story of Robin Hood, where a hacker steals from the rich corporations to give to the poor.
45. The animals in a city zoo start exhibiting human behaviors, and a zookeeper tries to find out why.
46. A character lives the same day over and over again and tries to find a way to break the cycle.

47. A world where children are born with knowledge of a certain profession, and a protagonist who wants to change theirs.
48. A story from the perspective of a tree that has lived for hundreds of years and has seen the world change around it.
49. A society where the concept of family doesn't exist, and people group together based on their skills and interests.
50. A detective who has the power to see the last thing a murder victim saw before they died.

Appendix B: 10 Screenplay Prompts

Screenplay Prompts:
1. A family dinner where each course reveals a new, escalating secret. How do the characters react to each revelation?
2. An AI has been elected as the mayor of a small town. How do the townspeople react and how does the AI handle human issues?
3. A couple is stuck in a time loop, reliving their wedding day. What do they discover about their relationship and themselves?
4. A world-renowned pianist has lost their ability to play. Show their journey as they relearn their passion and overcome their new obstacle.
5. A minor character from a classic work of fiction is given their own story. What's their perspective on the original events?
6. A heist takes place during a city-wide blackout. How does the darkness affect the thieves' plan and the pursuit by law enforcement?
7. A child gains the power to bring drawings to life. How does this power impact their life and those around them?
8. A person wakes up with a different body each day. How do they manage their relationships, job, and identity?
9. A forgotten mythical creature is found living in a metropolitan sewer system. What ensues when its existence is discovered by the public?
10. A character is gifted the ability to talk to objects. What do the objects reveal about the world and the people they interact with?

Appendix C: 10 Screenplay Prompts

Story Prompts:

1. The protagonist has the ability to taste the emotions of the person who cooked their food. How does this affect their life and relationships?
2. A famous city wakes up one morning to find all its landmarks have vanished. What's the impact on its residents and tourists?
3. A tree in a small town begins to grow currency instead of fruits. How does this impact the town and its inhabitants?
4. A character can hear everyone's thoughts, but only when they are lying. How do they use this skill in their daily life?
5. The world's first fully autonomous AI child has been created. How do they navigate human society and childhood?
6. Everyone has their future profession chosen at birth by a mystical entity. The protagonist is the first to reject their predetermined path.
7. The last dragon on earth disguises itself as a human to survive. What experiences do they have living amongst the species that hunted them?
8. A character has the ability to see a countdown timer above everyone's head, signifying how long they have left to live.
9. A magician discovers that their stage tricks are turning into real magic. How does this change their performances and life?
10. A society has found a way to eliminate sleep, leading to 24-hour days. How does this change the world and the protagonist's life?

Appendix D: 25 Editing Prompts

Editing Prompts:

1. The climax of the story feels rushed. How can you extend it and heighten the tension?
2. There are too many characters and it's confusing. Can you merge any characters or remove unnecessary ones?
3. The dialogue is unrealistic. How can you re-write it to sound more natural?
4. The pacing in the middle of the story is slow. How can you increase the pace while ensuring important details aren't lost?
5. There's a lot of telling, not showing. How can you demonstrate characters' feelings and events through actions and dialogue instead?
6. The main character is not likeable. How can you make them more relatable and sympathetic?
7. The narrative is hard to follow. How can you clarify the sequence of events or the motivations of the characters?
8. The story lacks vivid descriptions. How can you improve the language to help readers visualize the world and characters?
9. The ending is predictable. How can you introduce an unexpected twist that is still satisfying and makes sense?
10. The beginning of the story doesn't grab the reader's attention. How can you create a more engaging hook?
11. How can you introduce conflict early, or craft a unique scenario to captivate readers from the first page?
12. The conflict is resolved too easily. How can you introduce more obstacles or complications for the protagonist?
13. The villain's motives are unclear. How can you provide more insight into their actions and decisions?
14. The point of view shifts inconsistently. How can you make the transitions smoother or decide on a single perspective?
15. The world-building is inconsistent. How can you establish clearer rules for your universe and ensure they're adhered to?

16. The main character's development is not believable. How can you depict their growth in a more convincing way?
17. The theme of the story is unclear. How can you emphasize the underlying message more effectively?
18. The subplot does not add to the main plot. How can you make it more relevant or decide to remove it?
19. There's too much exposition in large chunks. How can you distribute this information more evenly and organically throughout the story?
20. The main character's goal is not compelling enough. How can you make their pursuit more urgent or significant?
21. Some scenes don't contribute to the plot. How can you revise or remove these to make every scene count?
22. The relationship between characters feels forced. How can you build their interactions more naturally?
23. The story relies too much on clichés. How can you give a fresh perspective or twist to familiar tropes?
24. The humor in the story falls flat. How can you make it more effective and in tune with the characters and situations?
25. The ending doesn't offer enough closure. How can you provide a more satisfying conclusion for your characters and readers?

Appendix E: 10 Sizing Prompts

Sizing Prompts

Here are some sizing prompts you can use for writing with AI:

1. Write a short story of approximately 500 words.
2. Write a chapter of about 1,000 words for a longer narrative.
3. Write a series of three chapters, with each chapter being around 1,500 words.
4. Write a novella consisting of 20,000 to 30,000 words.
5. Write a novel with a target length of 80,000 to 100,000 words.
6. Write a multi-volume epic spanning several books, with each book ranging from 150,000 to 200,000 words.
7. Write a flash fiction piece of around 250 words, capturing a complete story in a concise format.
8. Write a screenplay for a short film, aiming for approximately 15 to 20 pages.
9. Write a non-fiction article of about 2,000 words, exploring a specific topic or providing an informative analysis.
10. Write a series of interconnected short stories, with each story ranging from 3,000 to 5,000 words, creating a cohesive narrative arc.

Remember, these are just suggested sizes, and you can adjust them based on your specific needs. Additionally, when working on longer narratives, it's generally a good idea to break them down into smaller chapters or sections to maintain focus and quality in the writing process.

About the Author

Phill C. Akinwale, PMP, is a highly experienced project management professional with a proven track record in both government and private sectors. Throughout his career, he has worked with renowned companies such as Motorola, Honeywell, Emerson, Skillsoft, Citigroup, Iron Mountain, Brown and Caldwell, US Airways, and CVS Caremark, managing operational endeavors, projects, and project controls.

With his extensive knowledge and expertise in various facets of Project Management, Phill has become a trusted figure in the field. He has trained project management professionals worldwide, including prestigious organizations like NASA, FBI, USAF, USACE, US Army, and the Department of Transport. Over the past 15 years, he has provided training across five editions of the PMBOK® Guide, showcasing his commitment to staying up-to-date with industry standards.

Phill holds an impressive twelve project management certifications, with a notable focus on Agile Project Management. His certifications include Certified ScrumMaster (CSM), PMI Agile Certified Practitioner (PMI-ACP), Professional Scrum Master (PSM), Professional Scrum Product Owner (PSPO), Professional Agile Leadership (PAL), and Scaled Professional Scrum (SPS). This diverse range of certifications reflects his dedication to mastering various project management methodologies.

In addition to his project management expertise, Phill is a certified coach and speaker through the John Maxwell team. Leveraging his leadership and soft skills, he delivers impactful workshops, seminars, keynote speeches, and coaching sessions. He is passionate about guiding individuals, teams, and organizations in their desired direction, equipping them with the tools and knowledge to achieve their goals.

Phill is also a prolific author, having written over 20 books on a diverse range of topics. His written works cover areas such as bullying (including "The Bird Brained Bullies"), leadership, conflict resolution, time travel ("The Time Machine Project"), and even comics ("Project VBX 11"). Furthermore, he has created two short movies that explore themes of leadership drama in the workplace and project management.

With his vast experience, certifications, and passion for guiding others, Phill C. Akinwale, PMP, is a valuable asset to any organization or individual seeking project management expertise, leadership development, and personal growth.

In addition to his accomplishments in project management, writing, coaching, and speaking, Phill C. Akinwale, PMP, is also a talented musician. With a passion for creating music, Phill has released four albums and over 15 singles that showcase his artistic talent and creativity.

His musical works can be found under the name "Phill C" on popular music platforms such as Spotify, Apple Music, and other major music distribution channels. Whether it's his soulful melodies, captivating lyrics, or catchy beats, Phill's music resonates with listeners and offers a glimpse into his artistic expression.

Through his music, Phill C. Akinwale shares his unique perspective and emotions, creating an immersive experience for his audience. His musical endeavors add another dimension to his diverse portfolio, highlighting his versatility and passion for creativity in all its forms.

With his talent for project management, writing, coaching, speaking, and music, Phill C. Akinwale, PMP, is a multi-faceted professional who brings a wealth of expertise and creativity to every endeavor he undertakes.

Need the worksheets? Visit: http://models.praizionmedia.com or email: support@praizion.com